I Do? "Let's check"

Helga H.

MAPLE
PUBLISHERS

I Do? "Let's check"

Author: Helga H.

Copyright © Helga H. (2025)

The right of Helga H. to be identified as author of this work has been asserted by the author in accordance with section 77 and 78 of the Copyright, Designs and Patents Act 1983.

First Published in 2025

ISBN 978-1-83538-584-5 (Paperback)

Book layout by:
    White Magic Studios
    www.whitemagicstudios.co.uk

Book Cover by:
    Megan and Helga H.

Published by:
    Maple Publishers
    Fairbourne Drive, Atterbury,
    Milton Keynes,
    MK10 9RG, UK
    www.maplepublishers.com

A CIP catalogue record for this title is available from the British Library.

All rights reserved. No part of this book may be reproduced or translated by any form or by any means, electronic or mechanical, including photocopying, recording or by any information storage and retrieval system without written permission from the author.

The views expressed in this work are solely those of the author and do not reflect the opinions of Publishers, and the Publisher hereby disclaims any responsibility for them. This book should not be used as a substitute for the advice of a competent authority, admitted or authorized to advise on the subjects covered.

About The Author

Tina, who writes under her creative pseudonym Helga, was born in Milford Haven, Connecticut. A passionate lover of music, film, and art, she finds joy in creating and in spending meaningful time with the people she loves.

Through her creative work, Helga delves into the deeper meanings behind the choices we make and how those decisions are shaped by our early life experiences and the information we're given as we grow.

Her debut book, **I Do? "Let's check"**, is a thoughtful exploration of life commitments, inviting readers to reflect on the beliefs and motivations that guide our most important decisions.

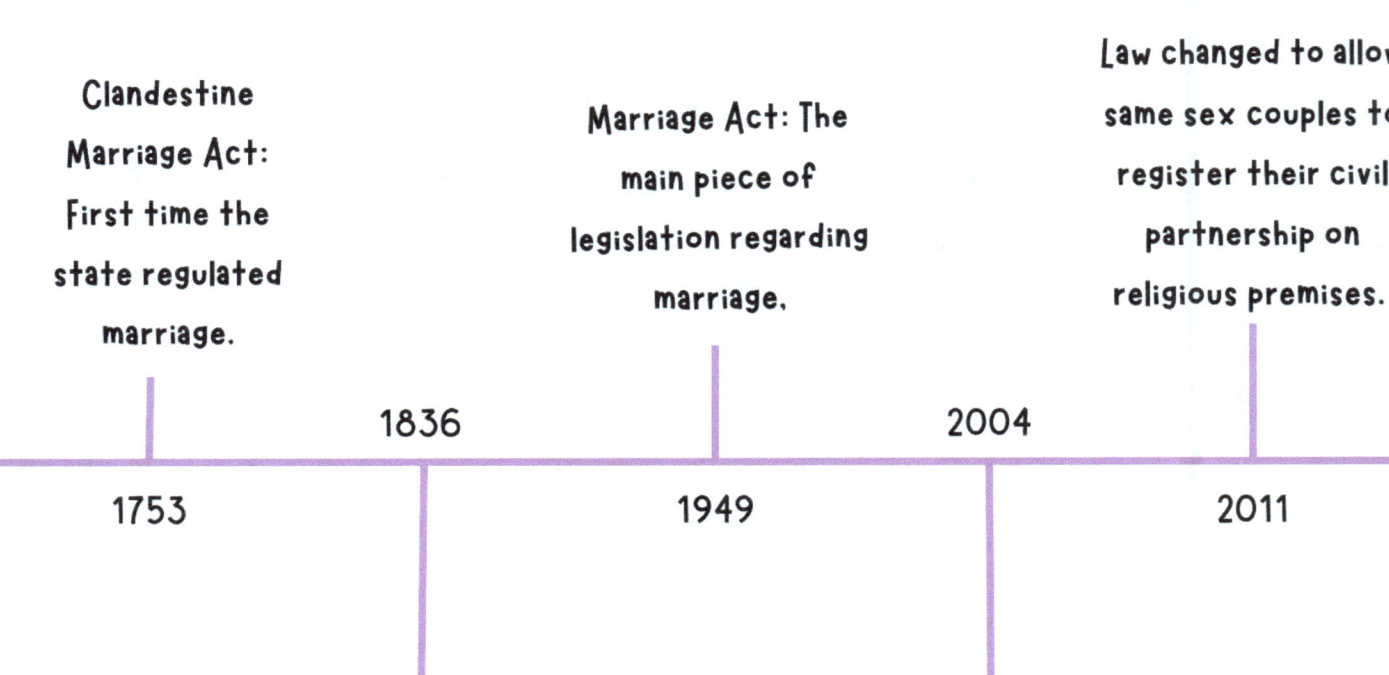

Marriage timeline

2012 — Public consultation on proposals to enable same sex couples to marry.

2012 — Government's response to consultation published, announcing commitment to enable same sex couples to marry.

2013 — Marriage (Same Sex Couples) Bill introduced into Parliament.

2013 — Marriage (Same Sex Couples) Act becomes law making equal marriage legal.

2014 — First same sex weddings to take place.

Contents

Dedication 07

Author's note and guide to **I Do? "Let's check"** 08

Introduction 11

Vows 15

One half of the quiz

Why are we getting married? 18

Love 20

Family 22

Communication 24

Finances 26

In-laws, outlaws and friends 28

Faith, Politics & Equal Rights 30

Chores 32

Scoring 34

Almost down the aisle 34

The beginning of your married life together 37

Your other half's half of the book (don't forget to flip!) 39

I Do? "Let's check"
Written By Helga H.

I dedicate this book to anyone out there who wants to give love and commitment a real good shot. To be curious about the person they want to spend the rest of their life with enough to take an hour or two out of a busy life to focus on the here and now – quiz style.

I thank everyone who has supported me on this book journey. I have had some top boss advice from friends and expert guidance from family. A special nod goes to Megan for her design details and patience, Elliott who originally brought the formatting to life and Abi for her motivational chats all the way from L.A. I appreciate you all.

FACT: Nothing in this world can take the place of persistence. Talent will not; nothing is more common than unsuccessful individuals with talent. Genius will not; unrewarded genius is almost a proverb. Education will not; the world is full of educated derelicts. Persistence and determination alone are omnipotent. - Ray Kroc, Grinding it Out.

Author's note and guide to I Do? "Let's check"

I Do "Let's check" is designed to be a fun questionnaire to do with your partner before taking a more formal commitment such as marriage or civil partnership. It's intended to be a shared book between two people with a light-hearted element which aims to unearth answers to questions you may have, or even to spark some new frank conversations. *I Do? "Let's check"* has been written to guide you smoothly towards the altar, and to keep as a reference book to remind each other of the commitments you gave.

The book is split in half: one for you, one for your other half. Work through the introductory sections together, sign your vows, and then pick a quiet moment and complete your half of the quiz on your own. Then it's hands off, over to your other half to do the same. No peeking is mandatory (yet!).

Then for the bit you've been waiting for:

Total up your **A**s, **B**s and **C**s, and then it's time to come together, share, chat, and maybe even learn something new about one another. The main objective of *I Do? "Let's check"* is to enjoy finding out more about each other's thoughts in an informal way, preparing you for a long and happy union.

Helga H.

FACT: A study conducted by Oxford University found that couples who actively participate in activities and games together are about 67% more likely to stay together.

"Love is like a precious plant, you can't just accept it and leave it in the cupboard or just think it's going to get on by itself. You've got to keep on watering on it, you've got to really look after it and nurture it."

-John Lennon

The I Do MOT

10 ideas to stick together like glue

1. Be friends. Be lovers.
2. Have your own views. Respect theirs too.
3. Find spontaneous things to do and do them often.
4. Be interested to keep them interested.
5. Remember those important anniversaries.
6. Support one another's passions.
7. Don't get frustrated. Be present.
8. Give each other privacy and respect boundaries.
9. Compliment the lovely things your spouse does.
10. Find a hobby or interest to have. Skydiving?

FACT: Studies suggest that couples who were friends first tend to have happier and more stable marriages.

Introduction

You've chosen your location, picked out the suits and dresses and practised the first dance. The rings have been sized, and the speeches prepared but... **STOP!**

Are you **100%** positive you know what married life will look like after the cases have been packed, the honeymoon is at an end, and you need to put the bins out and re-stock the fridge? Or will you be left feeling bereft, as famously sang by Freda Payne, "with just a band of gold".

Sooooo, to ensure you are in harmony and singing off the same hymn sheet why not take a little time as part of your preparations and glimpse into your future, with a series of multiple-choice questions that aim to tackle some of those niggling thoughts we want the answers to, but frankly don't want to ask.

Curious?

A – Maybe   **B** – Yes

If the answer is **A – Maybe**. We understand the confidence and trust needed to 'bare all' to one another. By embarking on this journey together, we hope to bring you answers to the niggling questions, creating a partnership that is founded on trust, love, and understanding.

If the answer is **B - Yes**, then what are you waiting for? Grab your spouse to be, find two pens and get quizzing on your way to a clearer future with great communication and a long-lasting partnership.

FACT: On the evening of her wedding to Prince Charles when Diana had cold feet, her sisters famously steadied her with the words, "too late Dutch, your face is already on the tea towels".

"I Do... Do You?"

"Should we do it?!"

"**I do**, do you?"

"I wasn't sure at first, but you smiled,
and somehow, so did I."

"Why?"

"Because it's **I DO** and it's with you."

It's not just a promise - it's a plan.

Soooo let's check off together

those As, Bs and Cs

to lead us to our totals,

with conversations of ease.

Let's make them clear,

And talk everything through.

Be honest.

Be brave.

And proceed with I Do.

                                             Anon. 2025

Vows

We are gathered here together on this page to witness the signing of the pre-nuptial agreement to complete

I Do? "Let's check"

Insert yours and yours truly names here:

I DO

.... & ....

Before we proceed do you agree to be each other's witness?

I DO

.... & ....

Do you both agree to complete your half of ***I Do? "Let's check"***?

I DO

.... & ....

Do you take this book to be your lawful wedded guide? To have and to hold from this quiz forward, for better or rocky times, for richer or no cashflow, in sickness and in wellness, to respect and to cherish until ***I Do "Let's check"*** can be archived?

I DO

.... & ....

Do you both agree to honour each other's honesty without judgement?

I DO

.... & ....

You may now proceed with ***I Do? "Let's check"***.

Suggestion – Why don't you check out a great song whilst you begin your quiz: 'For You' by Kenny Lattimore to get you in the mood!

FACT: A study by YouGov (2025) suggests two out of three women no longer take their partners name at marriage.

Some facts and figures
Ooohs and Aaahs

So, you've embarked on *I Do* and the faint sound of chapel bells are already ringing, but before we go any further here's a few facts about marriage that should raise a few **Ooohs** and **Aaahs**.

- **FACT 1:** *Approximately 250,000 lovely human couples utter "I Do" each year in the UK.* **Oooh.**

- **FACT 2:** *Since the implementation of the Marriage (Same Sex Couples) Act 2013, a total of 167,000 "I Do's" have taken place between same sex couples, replacing the original option of only a civil partnership.* **Aaah.**

- **FACT 3:** *58% of marriages are a success, but 42% end in divorce. We're talking approximately 30,000 divorce applications filed each year in the UK.* **Oooh.**

- **FACT 4:** *Most marriage bumps (ending in divorce) happen most commonly when couples have been married between 4 to 8 years (so just before you get your hands on your new bronze statue!).* **Aaah.**

Top tier reasons cited for divorce:

- **REASON 1:** *Infidelity*
- **REASON 2**: *Communication & connection*
- **REASON 3:** *Money troubles*

So, before you or yours truly run off with Brad Pitt and inherit seven stepchildren, or the bronze statue wedding gift gets mentioned in the Decree Nisi, let's get you talking about some of the issues that really matter.

And just a quick note to remember: DIY prenups are on the rise, but as James Joyce (famous author of Ulysses) famously uttered *"what's yours is mine and what's mine is my own"*.

FACT: A study by sociologist Nicholas Wolfinger found that the likelihood of divorce was lowest when a couple married between the ages of 28 and 32.

Get quizzing

Why are we getting married?

1. For one reason only and that is LOVE.
   - A. Yes, love is the reason and my only answer.
   - B. For other important reasons not just love.
   - C. I'm sure of my reasons but need to understand yours. Chat time?

2. Two is better than one.
   - A. Yes, I stopped wanting to be single when I met you.
   - B. Not necessarily but being on my own scares me.
   - C. Are we sure we are ready to give up singledom? Chat time perhaps.

3. The body clock is ticking.
   - A. Yes, no delays, we need to get a move on.
   - B. Kids? I'll keep my time free for now thanks (or maybe forever…)
   - C. Come to think of it, children have been on my mind recently. Time for a conversation?

4. We share a mini person already so getting married will show our commitment.
   - A. Yes, I am excited to be a formal family unit.
   - B. No, our commitment is proven already without the ceremony.
   - C. I think it would stop people asking us or feeling pressured, but I'd want to talk about if this is a worry to us or not! Chat time?

5. My mum has bought a formal hat and our family and friends are dropping hints.
   - A. Yes, they are but we are still marrying for our happiness.
   - B. Not hints, but I feel it's about time we tied the knot.
   - C. I've never thought to ask our families and friends opinion… maybe we should?

6. Two lots of rent, two lots of bills, this separate living is adding up.
   - A. Yes, it's expensive, but having extra cash is not my reason to marry you.
   - B. It does make better financial sense to combine forces.
   - C. Let's reaffirm that it is love versus convenience. Chat time?

FACT: A marriage ceremony typically ends with a kiss because in ancient Rome a kiss was a legal bond that sealed contracts, and marriage was seen as a contract.

Chat time notes

Love

1. Love to me is spending every moment together and never being apart.
   - A. Yes, that's what marriage and love mean to me.
   - B. No, love to me means we still value independence but trust each other when apart.
   - C. I would like to talk about what love means to both you and I. Chat time?

2. Do you think it's possible to always keep the flame of romance alight?
   - A. Yes, absolutely, with just a little thought and effort I do.
   - B. Hmmm. This could prove difficult. Let's make a deal to always remember birthdays and anniversaries.
   - C. I think we should share our thoughts on romantic expectations. Conversation?

3. How about a regular date night whereby we take turns to find an interesting activity to do?
   - A. Yes, great idea, planners at the ready.
   - B. Hmmm not necessary as we've bagged each other by then.
   - C. Ooh interesting idea - let's talk about making this a possibility?

4. Once married I'm sure bedroom antics will be replaced on occasions with other pastimes like scrolling. Can you cope not getting it on all the time?
   - A. Yes, because it's not the most important aspect in marriage.
   - B. Hmm… no, not really. If I'm honest, I thought more opportunities.
   - C. I think I'd like to talk about those expectations now. Chat time?

5. I might have an idea for role play or a secret fantasy. Should I tell you or just surprise you?
   - A. Surprise, surprise, yes! Couples who play together stay together.
   - B. No. Neither of these as I get embarrassed.
   - C. We've never talked role play or dressing up so perhaps it's time. Let's talk?

6. Write down three reasons why you love your other half:
   - ♡
   - ♡
   - ♡

FACT: Due to jobs, kids, TV, the internet, hobbies and home and family responsibilities, the average married couple spends just 4 minutes alone together each day.

Conversation notes

Family

1. After marriage would you like more than you and I? I'm talking little versions of us.
   - **A** Yes, I would, I can't wait!
   - **B** Hmmm, I'm not sure if there's room for more than the two of us?
   - **C** I'd like to clarify soon what both our inner thoughts are, chat time?

2. Let's imagine we can't conceive. Would you…
   - **A** Explore together the options on our table – whether that be IVF, egg/sperm donation, adopting, fostering or surrogacy?
   - **B** Want to spend some time independently reflecting on what feels most right to you, before joining forces and making a plan?
   - **C** I'd never considered any of these options before. Contemplation time needed.

3. If children aren't in our future plans (by choice or otherwise), would I want us to…
   - **A** Pursue our passions as one – whether it be travelling the world, climbing the ladder or taking up couple's rock climbing (anything goes)!
   - **B** Use that time to take on separate endeavours and value that independence from each other that we've always loved!
   - **C** Oh gosh… health permitting we might have a long road ahead with lots of free time… let's discuss how to spend it?

4. If having children is our path, would we…
   - **A** Start trying as soon as the honeymoon is over, let's go baby!
   - **B** No pressure on time, let's let nature take its course.
   - **C** A mutually convenient time decided by both of us. Planning chat?

5. Let's talk about our children from previous relationships. Will we manage and cope as one new extended family?
   - **A** Yes, we are a committed unit, and we will work as one (big!) team.
   - **B** I'm not sure how this will work practically with our resources.
   - **C** I would like to discuss the logistics further with you. Conversation time?

Note: If not applicable feel free to skip ahead! For blended family support, check out: www.helpguide.org.

6. Stay at home vs. the workplace. Should we divide up and conquer both roles equally?
   - **A** Yes, I like the idea of us combining job share and parenting equally – bring on the dream team!
   - **B** No, as I believe a set role for each of us will make it easier.
   - **C** How about we draw up a five-year future proof plan? Chat time?

FACT: Children raised in two-parent families have on average, higher academic achievements, better emotional health and fewer behavioural problems.

Contemplation notes

Communication

1. I want to tell you anything and everything, whatever it is or whenever it is.
   - **A** Yes, being free to express my thoughts is a huge plus.
   - **B** Not everything no, as some discussions are personal and difficult to navigate (or best between friends not lovers!).
   - **C** Should we set time in our weekly schedule to open up at conversation time?

2. Love birds that we are but let's face it, sometimes we will irritate each other. Do we deal with it immediately?
   - **A** Yes, all cards out on the table, transparency is key.
   - **B** No, sometimes it's easier to leave muddy waters alone and let it pass.
   - **C** I'd like to find a cute way now to complain about you, maybe a sticky note complaint system? Thoughts?

3. There's an issue and its a big one (like family or finances), is discussing it together the best way to resolve the problem?
   - **A** Yes. Talking it through and tackling as one is always the best way to reach resolve.
   - **B** Not always, let's let the drama die down a bit – we don't always both need to get involved.
   - **C** We should talk about how we should solve problems as a couple. Chat time?

4. Addicted to chocolate, yes, but let's imagine an addiction develops to something more serious. Would you confide in me?
   - **A** Yes, I trust you completely. I can tell you everything, even when it's a tricky topic.
   - **B** No, I feel I would get professional help first and then tell you.
   - **C** I'd like us to define what addiction means to each of us and make time to chat about this.

4. Sometimes I dream of us packing it all in and moving to another country. No matter how crazy an idea may seem, will you always share your goals with me?
   - **A** Yes, you are my teammate, so we dream and plan together.
   - **B** No, not if I think you will find it silly or impractical.
   - **C** I'm not sure I know all your dreams. Cuddle up dreaming time under the stars perhaps?

5. Labour vs. Tories? Organic vs. farmed? Matters that may affect the welfare of our family and our future I think should be up for debate.
   - **A** Yes, love it. Weekly family meeting?
   - **B** No not really, as individual opinions matter and should be mutually respected if you feel strongly enough.
   - **C** I'd like if we could talk of big potential differences in opinions now. Chat time?

FACT: Words form only 7% of our communication to anyone including spouses. Tone of voice accounts for 38% and body language is responsible for 55% of the message's spouses receive from each other.

Chat time notes

Finances

1. "Money talk honey", should we join up our accounts or keep them separate?
   - A. All in the pot for me - I prefer joint accounts for everything.
   - B. I believe we should keep our earnings separate.
   - C. Hmmm. I'd like it if we could talk about a good compromise to this? Conversation time?

2. "Splashing the cash", what do you think about having a spending and saving allowance? Good idea?
   - A. Yes, great idea, let's set these accounts up if we haven't already!
   - B. I think we can both be trusted to manage our own money honey.
   - C. We should talk about a financial system that suits us both. Chats?

3. Monthly bills have come around ☹. Do we share the responsibility?
   - A. Yes, let's divide up who's paying what, when and how (direct debit's all the way!).
   - B. No. I think it would be better done by whichever one of us is more organised.
   - C. Are we totally transparent on our finances? Let's talk about money more.

4. Future plans and goals: are we open to support each other through potential financial changes? I'm talking opening a coffee shop or going back to college.
   - A. Yes, we scheme together and dream together.
   - B. No, I'm not sure if we would ever be in a strong enough financial position to dream this big.
   - C. I'd like us to discuss any unfulfilled dreams and goals. Conversation time?

5. "For richer or for poorer". Lottery winner or credit rating at an all-time low. Ready to confess?
   - A. Yes, I'm ready to show my financial cards on the table. No judgement just honesty.
   - B. No, I don't want to talk about money. Finances scare me and I prefer to keep some things private.
   - C. I'm up for a financial check-up with you. Let's have an open and honest chat?

6. I'm up for future financial planning, I'm talking pensions partner.
   - A. I'm on board, it's important to save for our future together.
   - B. I'm not worried about planning this far ahead just yet … let's enjoy spending whilst we can.
   - C. Taking some financial advice wouldn't hurt us if you agree… conversation time?

FACT: Compared to singles, married people accumulate about four times more savings and assets.

Conversation notes

In-laws, Outlaws & Friends

1. The Kardashians we are not, but is spending time seeing respective families important to you?
   - **A** Yes, our families are very important to me so it's crucial we make time.
   - **B** No, I'm not that fussed about visiting each other's relatives too frequently to be honest.
   - **C** It would be good to talk about respecting each other's needs for family time, let's discuss?

2. "My mums this Sunday, yours the following week?". Is it good to divide up special holidays and celebrations between families?
   - **A** Yes, I think this is important to maintain strong bonds and make sure no one is left out.
   - **B** No, not necessarily as we will have our own family traditions in place.
   - **C** I'd like a chat now about dividing up special holidays between us. Conversation?

3. "You choose your friends, not your family". Is maintaining good relationships with mates once married healthy in a relationship?
   - **A** It's not as crucial as we'll have each other for support, but I wouldn't want to lose touch either.
   - **B** Yes, it's important to me to have a support network beyond just you and I.
   - **C** I'd like a chat about who is important to us and how we stay committed to friends. Time to talk?

4. "Let's paint the town red". Are nights out with our own friends still on the cards once we're married?
   - **A** My friends are your friends, let's hit the dancefloor together!
   - **B** It's great to see each other having fun and some down time. I'll keep your side of the bed warm until you get home!
   - **C** I'd like to set some realistic expectations for maintaining time for personal friendships. Conversation?

5. Friend or foe? Sticking their noses in our business and it's starting to affect us. Should I tell you or sort it myself?
   - **A** Yes, I'd tell you, I want us to always be honest with each other about conflict.
   - **B** No, I'd sort it out myself by speaking to the person causing waves, I don't need to always get you involved.
   - **C** Let's talk together about our own loyalties and responsibilities to others. Chat time?

6. "Any room at the inn?". Someone close to us needs some support. Are you comfortable opening the doors to our home?
   - **A** Yes, if we can help a friend or relative in need it's all hands on deck.
   - **B** No, I'm not too keen on our house having an open-door policy if I'm honest.
   - **C** Let's discuss this possibility to smooth the way if this happens in our future?

***FACT**: 81% of happily married couples said partners, friends and family rarely interfered with the relationship, compared to just 38% of unhappy couples.*

Contemplation notes

Faith, Politics & Equal Rights

1. Buddhist, Christian, Muslim, Catholic, Atheist or Faerie faith. Are having similar beliefs crucial for wedded bliss?

   A. Yes, sharing beliefs that bind together our values will strengthen our union.
   B. Not really. You have your belief, I have mine. Harmony will reign if we keep it that way.
   C. We've not discussed our beliefs enough. Chat time?

2. I believe in Faries, you believe in a higher being. Can our interfaith union stand the test of time?

   A. Yes. Supporting one another's individual beliefs will fortify our teamwork
   B. Our beliefs don't need to merge as one to make our alliance a success.
   C. Let's take the time to look into our interfaith future. More conversation?

3. One leans to the left and one to the right. Can we reach a political middle ground by leaning towards each other?

   A. Yes. Sharing and compromising on ideals is a fair and balanced vote from me.
   B. Hmmm. Not sure as I'll follow the leader that ticks all my boxes.
   C. I'd like to chat more on how our political stances may impact our coupledom.

4. Rally's, Sunday services, prayers or meditation.
   Are rituals that require personal time up for negotiation?

   A. Yes. Negotiable. We make room to support one another's customs special to us.
   B. Non-negotiable. Having that time and space to focus on myself is vital.
   C. Let's contemplate this and get back to one another. Conversation time?

5. Baptism, Christenings, Humanist or Bar Mitzvah. Who chooses the faith for our family? **I Do**, you do or they do? **Let's check**.

   A. Yes, we do. Practicing and believing in a faith we have chosen will pave our foundation.
   B. They do. Let our family decide on a faith. If any, in their own time.
   C. Our differences in our beliefs might need a deeper conversation. Contemplation time?

   Note: If not applicable feel free to skip to question 6

6. Faith, Politics and Equal Rights. Can we blend all three into a smoothie full of equality?

   A. Yes. A unit is a unit and the more diverse and blended the mix the healthier our partnership tastes.
   B. Not necessarily as blending might compromise individual views true to our oneself.
   C. I feel we could dig deeper into these three ingredients to help serve up more truths. Note time?

FACT: *Research indicates that couples who share similar political and religious beliefs tend to have more stable relationships.*

Conversation notes

Chores

1. Gloves at the ready. Are you up for tackling the loo?

   - **A** Yes, this is my domain. Leave me to the cleaning because we balance responsibilities well.
   - **B** No, it's an awful job, no hands up from me.
   - **C** I think it's time to decide on who attacks the bins and bathrooms. Chat time?

2. If cleaning fairies don't exist, should we work out how we tidy the gaff between us?

   - **A** Yes, we do it together like we do everything else. The A team.
   - **B** I don't want to do any cleaning! I hate it! I value free time - I think we should hire a cleaner.
   - **C** We need to talk more about fairly dividing up tasks, conversation?

3. Click and collect the weekly shop or trolleys at the ready for supermarket sweep?

   - **A** We're both logical, practical time-savers. Let's do it online unless we urgently need milk or chocolate and we nip out together!
   - **B** It's easier and more efficient if one of us takes on this task each week.
   - **C** I'd like us to discuss options that suit us both and make life easier. Chat time?

4. Head chef of the house. Is it better a role shared, or first through the door gets the hob on?

   - **A** Yes, shared. Cooking is much nicer when done together.
   - **B** It makes sense to me that first one home gets preppin'. *P.S, this isn't an excuse to take the long way home…*
   - **C** We've usually managed well, but not a bad idea to do a cooking rota planner. Conversation time?

5. Chief dishwasher or chief tidy upper. Is it easier to assign each of us a role to get the job done?

   - **A** Let's get the job done together, hit go on our favourite playlist and shimmy around the kitchen!
   - **B** I think we assign roles – how about the cook never washes up, and chief tidy upper takes on the bins?
   - **C** How about we make time to talk about our favourite home tasks over our favourite lasagne? Chat time?

6. D.I.Y. maintenance and flat packs. Own up, who's good with a hammer and nail?

   - **A** Together I vow to build a foundation with you. Brick by brick, flatpack by flatpack and screw by screw, as long as I'm doing it with you.
   - **B** No, count me out! You find your way around a spirit level better than I do. This is your home turf.
   - **C** Finding a local handyman is appealing to me right now! Conversation on this?

FACT: *Research consistently shows that women continue to do more household chores than men, even in relationships where both partners work.*

Chat time notes

Almost Down the Aisle

Finished? Both ready? Time to do the maths.

Before you do, here's a quick guide to the **A**'s **B**'s and **C**'s to help summarising a breeze:

A's: If you've got mostly **A**'s you're ready and willing to dive in the deep end. You're ready to jump out that plane, skydive together, trusting your partner is there with the safety net.

B's: Mostly **B**'s means you thrive on independent thinking, meaning your own safety net is safely packed ready before your partner gives their thumbs up too.

C's: Lots of C's indicates cinema trips could be on hold for now in place of needing time to chatter, natter and chatter some more. C really does stand for **conversation**!

Insert yours and yours truly names here:

.... & ....

TOTAL number of A's:

Compatible on mostly **A**'s? **A**'s from you and **A**'s from your other half doesn't in this case stand for car membership, but a direct debit to a thinking on the same page great marriage contract.

.... & ....

TOTAL number of B's:

Both scoring mostly **B**'s? That reveals you both thrive on a bit of independence, but you won't get stung in this union if you allow compromise to play a greater role, especially when it comes to making decisions as important as which kitchen paint sample makes the cut!

.... & ....

TOTAL number of C's:

C is the symbol for the speed of light, but you two aren't dashing off just yet as your frankness is propelling you into the **C** zone - MORE CONVERSATION!

.... & ....

Quiz Complete, Maths Complete, What Now?!

The small print: you must agree on **1**, **2** or **3**.

1. Book down, take a break, do the funky chicken, then when you both are ready cosy up for a whys and wherefores on the **A**'s, the **B**'s and the **C**'s to hopefully land on us dotting the I's and crossing the T's.

2. Find a hideaway place for now for both completed halves of **I DO** *'Let's check' (no peeking)* and set out a time mutually agreeable for both to sit down and reveal your answers. Remember that safety net?

3. Time capsule or safe that can store your book and answers **ONLY** to be opened by agreement either or at the event of:

Option A: 7 years and 2 months

At this point, you'll have passed the average time to stay wed, so crack open the champagne!

Option B: Your 50th wedding anniversary

*You've cracked the code to a long and happy wedded life. It's now time to share the secrets in your own book called '**We made it**, because we checked it'.*

FACT: The seven-year itch is a myth - a study found that couples who stay married for seven years are likely to be together for good.

"There is no more lovely, friendly, and charming relationship, communion or company than a good marriage"

-Martin Luther King

Here's to the beginning of your committed life together...

You've ticked the boxes, done the maths and either discussed or planned to have conversations on the whys and wherefores of your reasons for your **A**'s, **B**'s and **C**'s and I'm sure that you will probably know one or two more facts about your partner than when you embarked on, **I Do *'Let's check'*.**

Sooooooooo Celebrate!

As it's common knowledge that the ability to talk and listen to each other is key to a healthy marriage you two are already on course for a great future together, and just to cement it the New York Times concluded that...

"Being married makes people happier and more satisfied with their lives than those who remain single."

NO ENTRY

What did I say... No peeking!

That time notes

42

Chores

1. Gloves at the ready. Are you up for tackling the loo?

A Yes, this is my domain. Leave me to the cleaning because we balance responsibilities well.

B No, it's an awful job, no hands up from me.

C I think it's time to decide on who attacks the bins and bathrooms. Chat time?

2. If cleaning fairies don't exist, should we work out how we tidy the gaff between us?

A Yes, we do it together like we do everything else. The A team.

B I don't want to do any cleaning! I hate it! I value free time - I think we should hire a cleaner.

C We need to talk more about fairly dividing up tasks, conversation?

3. Click and collect the weekly shop or trolleys at the ready for supermarket sweep?

A We're both logical, practical time-savers. Let's do it online unless we urgently need milk or chocolate and we nip out together!

B It's easier and more efficient if one of us takes on this task each week.

C I'd like us to discuss options that suit us both and make life easier. Chat time?

4. Head chef of the house. Is it better a role shared, or first through the door gets the hob on?

A Yes, shared. Cooking is much nicer when done together.

B It makes sense to me that first one home gets preppin'. *P.S, this isn't an excuse to take the long way home…*

C We've usually managed well, but not a bad idea to do a cooking rota planner. Conversation time?

5. Chief dishwasher or chief tidy upper. Is it easier to assign each of us a role to get the job done?

A Let's get the job done together, hit go on our favourite playlist and shimmy around the kitchen!

B I think we assign roles – how about the cook never washes up, and chief tidy upper takes on the bins?

C How about we make time to talk about our favourite home tasks over our favourite lasagne? Chat time?

6. D.I.Y. maintenance and flat packs. Own up, who's good with a hammer and nail?

A Together I vow to build a foundation with you. Brick by brick, flatpack by flatpack and screw by screw, as long as I'm doing it with you.

B No, count me out! You find your way around a spirit level better than I do. This is your home turf.

C Finding a local handyman is appealing to me right now! Conversation on this?

FACT: Research consistently shows that women continue to do more household chores than men, even in relationships where both partners work.

43

Conversation notes

Faith, Politics & Equal Rights

1. Buddhist, Christian, Muslim, Catholic, Atheist or Faerie faith. Are having similar beliefs crucial for wedded bliss?

A Yes, sharing beliefs that bind together our values will strengthen our union.

B Not really. You have your belief, I have mine. Harmony will reign if we keep it that way.

C We've not discussed our beliefs enough. Chat time?

2. I believe in Faries, you believe in a higher being. Can our interfaith union stand the test of time?

A Yes. Supporting one another's individual beliefs will fortify our teamwork

B Our beliefs don't need to merge as one to make our alliance a success.

C Let's take the time to look into our interfaith future. More conversation?

3. One leans to the left and one to the right. Can we reach a political middle ground by leaning towards each other?

A Yes. Sharing and compromising on ideals is a fair and balanced vote from me.

B Hmmm. Not sure as I'll follow the leader that ticks all my boxes.

C I'd like to chat more on how our political stances may impact our coupledom.

4. Rally's, Sunday services, prayers or meditation.
Are rituals that require personal time up for negotiation?

A Yes. Negotiable. We make room to support one another's customs special to us.

B Non-negotiable. Having that time and space to focus on myself is vital.

C Let's contemplate this and get back to one another. Conversation time?

5. Baptism, Christenings, Humanist or Bar Mitzvah. Who chooses the faith for our family? **I Do**, you do or they do? **Let's check**.

A Yes, we do. Practicing and believing in a faith we have chosen will pave our foundation.

B They do. Let our family decide on a faith. If any, in their own time.

C Our differences in our beliefs might need a deeper conversation. Contemplation time?

Note: If not applicable feel free to skip to question 6

6. Faith, Politics and Equal Rights. Can we blend all three into a smoothie full of equality?

A Yes. A unit is a unit and the more diverse and blended the mix the healthier our partnership tastes.

B Not necessarily as blending might compromise individual views true to our oneself.

C I feel we could dig deeper into these three ingredients to help serve up more truths. Note time?

FACT: Research indicates that couples who share similar political and religious beliefs tend to have more stable relationships.

Contemplation notes

In-laws, Outlaws & Friends

1. The Kardashians we are not, but is spending time seeing respective families important to you?

A Yes, our families are very important to me so it's crucial we make time.

B No, I'm not that fussed about visiting each other's relatives too frequently to be honest.

C It would be good to talk about respecting each other's needs for family time, let's discuss?

2. "My mums this Sunday, yours the following week?". Is it good to divide up special holidays and celebrations between families?

A Yes, I think this is important to maintain strong bonds and make sure no one is left out.

B No, not necessarily as we will have our own family traditions in place.

C I'd like a chat now about dividing up special holidays between us. Conversation?

3. "You choose your friends, not your family". Is maintaining good relationships with mates once married healthy in a relationship?

A It's not as crucial as we'll have each other for support, but I wouldn't want to lose touch either.

B Yes, it's important to me to have a support network beyond just you and I.

C I'd like a chat about who is important to us and how we stay committed to friends. Time to talk?

4. "Let's paint the town red". Are nights out with our own friends still on the cards once we're married?

A My friends are your friends, let's hit the dancefloor together!

B It's great to see each other having fun and some down time. I'll keep your side of the bed warm until you get home!

C I'd like to set some realistic expectations for maintaining time for personal friendships. Conversation?

5. Friend or foe? Sticking their noses in our business and it's starting to affect us. Should I tell you or sort it myself?

A Yes, I'd tell you, I want us to always be honest with each other about conflict.

B No, I'd sort it out myself by speaking to the person causing waves, I don't need to always get you involved.

C Let's talk together about our own loyalties and responsibilities to others. Chat time?

6. "Any room at the inn?". Someone close to us needs some support. Are you comfortable opening the doors to our home?

A Yes, if we can help a friend or relative in need it's all hands on deck.

B No, I'm not too keen on our house having an open-door policy if I'm honest.

C Let's discuss this possibility to smooth the way if this happens in our future?

FACT: 81% of happily married couples said partners, friends and family rarely interfered with the relationship, compared to just 38% of unhappy couples.

Conversation notes

Finances

1. "Money talk honey", should we join up our accounts or keep them separate?

A All in the pot for me - I prefer joint accounts for everything.

B I believe we should keep our earnings separate.

C Hmmm. I'd like it if we could talk about a good compromise to this? Conversation time?

2. "Splashing the cash", what do you think about having a spending and saving allowance? Good idea?

A Yes, great idea, let's set these accounts up if we haven't already!

B I think we can both be trusted to manage our own money honey.

C We should talk about a financial system that suits us both. Chats?

3. Monthly bills have come around ☹. Do we share the responsibility?

A Yes, let's divide up who's paying what, when and how (direct debit's all the way!).

B No. I think it would be better done by whichever one of us is more organised.

C Are we totally transparent on our finances? Let's talk about money more.

4. Future plans and goals: are we open to support each other through potential financial changes? I'm talking opening a coffee shop or going back to college.

A Yes, we scheme together and dream together.

B No, I'm not sure if we would ever be in a strong enough financial position to dream this big.

C I'd like us to discuss any unfulfilled dreams and goals. Conversation time?

5. "For richer or for poorer". Lottery winner or credit rating at an all-time low. Ready to confess?

A Yes, I'm ready to show my financial cards on the table. No judgement just honesty.

B No, I don't want to talk about money. Finances scare me and I prefer to keep some things private.

C I'm up for a financial check-up with you. Let's have an open and honest chat?

6. I'm up for future financial planning, I'm talking pensions partner.

A I'm on board, it's important to save for our future together.

B I'm not worried about planning this far ahead just yet … let's enjoy spending whilst we can.

C Taking some financial advice wouldn't hurt us if you agree… conversation time?

FACT: Compared to singles, married people accumulate about four times more savings and assets.

49

Chat time notes

Communication

1. I want to tell you anything and everything, whatever it is or whenever it is.

A Yes, being free to express my thoughts is a huge plus.

B Not everything no, as some discussions are personal and difficult to navigate (or best between friends not lovers!).

C Should we set time in our weekly schedule to open up at conversation time?

2. Love birds that we are but let's face it, sometimes we will irritate each other. Do we deal with it immediately?

A Yes, all cards out on the table, transparency is key.

B No, sometimes it's easier to leave muddy waters alone and let it pass.

C I'd like to find a cute way now to complain about you, maybe a sticky note complaint system? Thoughts?

3. There's an issue and its a big one (like family or finances), is discussing it together the best way to resolve the problem?

A Yes. Talking it through and tackling as one is always the best way to reach resolve.

B Not always, let's let the drama die down a bit – we don't always both need to get involved.

C We should talk about how we should solve problems as a couple. Chat time?

4. Addicted to chocolate, yes, but let's imagine an addiction develops to something more serious. Would you confide in me?

A Yes, I trust you completely. I can tell you everything, even when it's a tricky topic.

B No, I feel I would get professional help first and then tell you.

C I'd like us to define what addiction means to each of us and make time to chat about this.

4. Sometimes I dream of us packing it all in and moving to another country. No matter how crazy an idea may seem, will you always share your goals with me?

A Yes, you are my teammate, so we dream and plan together.

B No, not if I think you will find it silly or impractical.

C I'm not sure I know all your dreams. Cuddle up dreaming time under the stars perhaps?

5. Labour vs. Tories? Organic vs. farmed? Matters that may affect the welfare of our family and our future I think should be up for debate.

A Yes, love it. Weekly family meeting?

B No not really, as individual opinions matter and should be mutually respected if you feel strongly enough.

C I'd like if we could talk of big potential differences in opinions now. Chat time?

FACT: Words form only 7% of our communication to anyone including spouses. Tone of voice accounts for 38% and body language is responsible for 55% of the message's spouses receive from each other.

Contemplation notes

Family

1. After marriage would you like more than you and I? I'm talking little versions of us.

A	Yes, I would, I can't wait!
B	Hmmm, I'm not sure if there's room for more than the two of us?
C	I'd like to clarify soon what both our inner thoughts are, chat time?

2. Let's imagine we can't conceive. Would you…

A	Explore together the options on our table – whether that be IVF, egg/sperm donation, adopting, fostering or surrogacy?
B	Want to spend some time independently reflecting on what feels most right to you, before joining forces and making a plan?
C	I'd never considered any of these options before. Contemplation time needed.

3. If children aren't in our future plans (by choice or otherwise), would I want us to…

A	Pursue our passions as one – whether it be travelling the world, climbing the ladder or taking up couple's rock climbing (anything goes)!
B	Use that time to take on separate endeavours and value that independence from each other that we've always loved!
C	Oh gosh… health permitting we might have a long road ahead with lots of free time… let's discuss how to spend it?

4. If having children is our path, would we…

A	Start trying as soon as the honeymoon is over, let's go baby!
B	No pressure on time, let's let nature take its course.
C	A mutually convenient time decided by both of us. Planning chat?

5. Let's talk about our children from previous relationships. Will we manage and cope as one new extended family?

A	Yes, we are a committed unit, and we will work as one (big!) team.
B	I'm not sure how this will work practically with our resources.
C	I would like to discuss the logistics further with you. Conversation time?

Note: If not applicable feel free to skip ahead! For blended family support, check out: www.helpguide.org.

6. Stay at home vs. the workplace. Should we divide up and conquer both roles equally?

A	Yes, I like the idea of us combining job share and parenting equally – bring on the dream team!
B	No, as I believe a set role for each of us will make it easier.
C	How about we draw up a five-year future proof plan? Chat time?

FACT: Children raised in two-parent families have on average, higher academic achievements, better emotional health and fewer behavioural problems.

53

Conversation notes

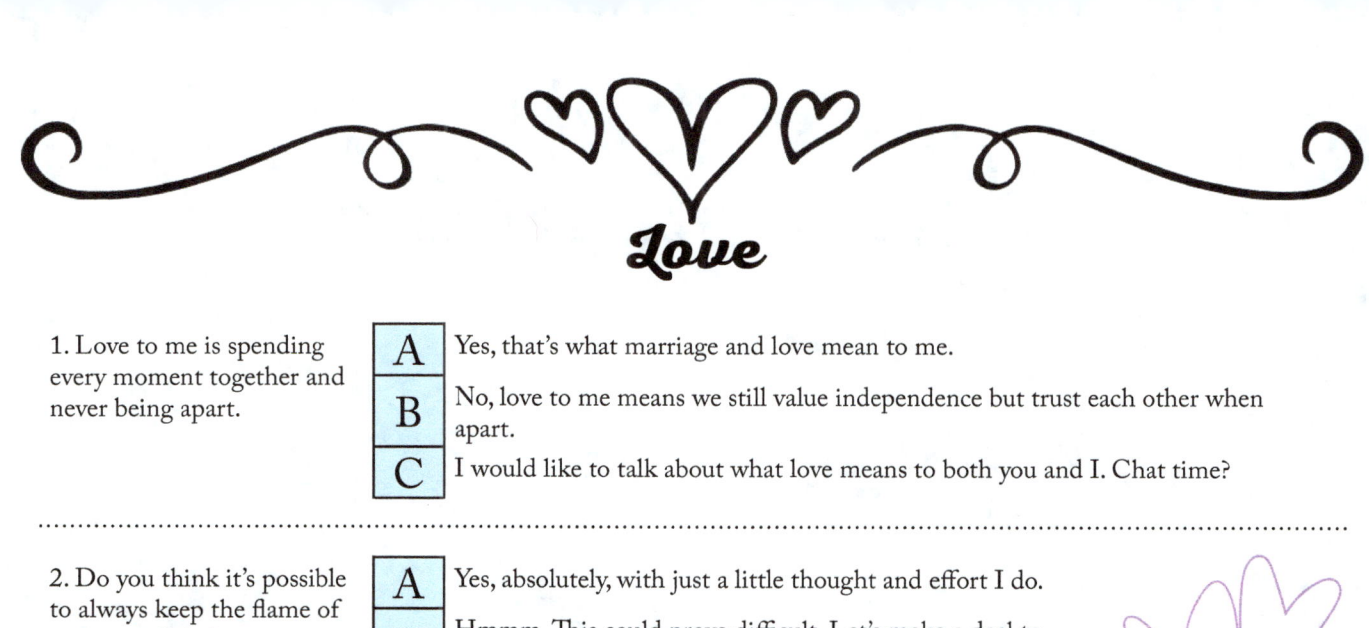

Love

1. Love to me is spending every moment together and never being apart.

A	Yes, that's what marriage and love mean to me.
B	No, love to me means we still value independence but trust each other when apart.
C	I would like to talk about what love means to both you and I. Chat time?

2. Do you think it's possible to always keep the flame of romance alight?

A	Yes, absolutely, with just a little thought and effort I do.
B	Hmmm. This could prove difficult. Let's make a deal to always remember birthdays and anniversaries.
C	I think we should share our thoughts on romantic expectations. Conversation?

3. How about a regular date night whereby we take turns to find an interesting activity to do?

A	Yes, great idea, planners at the ready.
B	Hmmm not necessary as we've bagged each other by then.
C	Ooh interesting idea - let's talk about making this a possibility?

4. Once married I'm sure bedroom antics will be replaced on occasions with other pastimes like scrolling. Can you cope not getting it on all the time?

A	Yes, because it's not the most important aspect in marriage.
B	Hmm… no, not really. If I'm honest, I thought more opportunities.
C	I think I'd like to talk about those expectations now. Chat time?

5. I might have an idea for role play or a secret fantasy. Should I tell you or just surprise you?

A	Surprise, surprise, yes! Couples who play together stay together.
B	No. Neither of these as I get embarrassed.
C	We've never talked role play or dressing up so perhaps it's time. Let's talk?

6. Write down three reasons why you love your other half:

FACT: Due to jobs, kids, TV, the internet, hobbies and home and family responsibilities, the average married couple spends just 4 minutes alone together each day.

Chat time notes

Why are we getting married?

1. For one reason only and that is LOVE.

- **A** Yes, love is the reason and my only answer.
- **B** For other important reasons not just love.
- **C** I'm sure of my reasons but need to understand yours. Chat time?

2. Two is better than one.

- **A** Yes, I stopped wanting to be single when I met you.
- **B** Not necessarily but being on my own scares me.
- **C** Are we sure we are ready to give up singledom? Chat time perhaps.

3. The body clock is ticking.

- **A** Yes, no delays, we need to get a move on.
- **B** Kids? I'll keep my time free for now thanks (or maybe forever…)
- **C** Come to think of it, children have been on my mind recently. Time for a conversation?

4. We share a mini person already so getting married will show our commitment.

- **A** Yes, I am excited to be a formal family unit.
- **B** No, our commitment is proven already without the ceremony.
- **C** I think it would stop people asking us or feeling pressured, but I'd want to talk about if this is a worry to us or not! Chat time?

5. My mum has bought a formal hat and our family and friends are dropping hints.

- **A** Yes, they are but we are still marrying for our happiness.
- **B** Not hints, but I feel it's about time we tied the knot.
- **C** I've never thought to ask our families and friends opinion… maybe we should?

6. Two lots of rent, two lots of bills, this separate living is adding up.

- **A** Yes, it's expensive, but having extra cash is not my reason to marry you.
- **B** It does make better financial sense to combine forces.
- **C** Let's reaffirm that it is love versus convenience. Chat time?

FACT: A marriage ceremony typically ends with a kiss because in ancient Rome a kiss was a legal bond that sealed contracts, and marriage was seen as a contract.

Get quizzing!

59

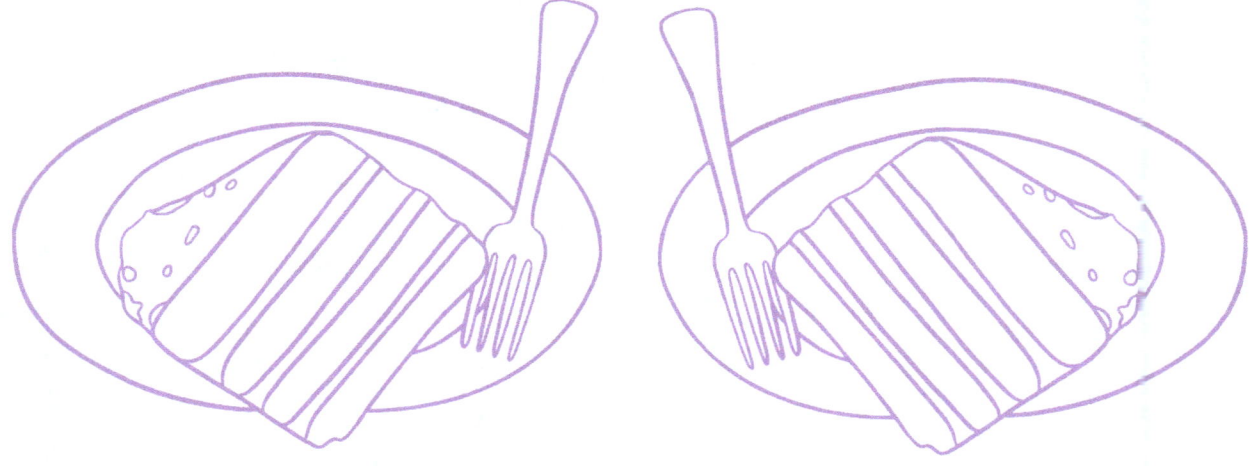

Any forks on this marital path?
Don't delay.
It's your turn.
Your half.
Your answer.

"I Do?" Let's check

Helga H.

MAPLE
PUBLISHERS

www.ingramcontent.com/pod-product-compliance
Lightning Source LLC
Chambersburg PA
CBHW051423070526
44584CB00023B/3562